Hans Brinkmann
Oliver Gray

# Avoiding Mistakes

## A Practice Book for Intermediate Learners

**Key + Index**



Diesterweg

Hans Brinkmann
Oliver Gray

# Avoiding Mistakes

## A Practice Book for Intermediate Learners

**Key + Index**





Druck A[3] / Jahr 2014
Alle Drucke der Serie A sind im Unterricht parallel verwendbar.

Redaktion: Demet Kömür
Herstellung: Harald Thumser, Frankfurt am Main
Satz: Stahringer Satz GmbH, Grünberg
Druck und Bindung: Westermann Druck Zwickau GmbH

ISBN 978-3-425-**00442**-6

# KEY TO THE EXERCISES

The answers offered in the key are the most appropriate though not in all cases the only acceptable ones. Alternatives are given in brackets, but these cannot always exhaust all the possibilities.
The page numbers are given in the symbol on the left.

# I. SPELLING

## A. Difficult Words

### 1. Frequently Confused Words

11

**a) a** *or* **e***?*
1. then, than; 2. marry, merry; 3. affect, effect; 4. effort, afford; 5. expect, accepted

**b) ea** *or* **ee***?*
1. beer, bear; 2. sweat, sweet; 3. great, greeted, great; 4. speech, speak; 5. deeds, dead

**c) e** *or* **not***?*
1. height; 2. costumes; 3. customs; 4. quite, quiet; 5. bath, bathe; 6. breath, breathe

**d) oa, oo, ou, au, o** *or …?*
1. coast; 2. loose, lose; 3. soup, soap; 4. course, cause

**e) shirt** *or* **skirt***, etc.?*
1. skirt, shirt; 2. Channel, Canal; 3. mayor, officials; 4. last, repaired, least; 5. last, least

**f) its / it's, whose / who's, there / their / they're***?*
1. who's, it's; 2. its, it's; 3. who's, whose; 4. who's, whose; 5. their, there, they're

### 2. Words with Special Consonants

13

**a) One or two consonants?**
1. success – occurrence – occasion – necessary – accident – to accompany
2. shadow – address – body
3. metal – gallery – model – really
4. immediate – committee – programme
5. apartment – copy – to disappear – opportunity – to apply – disappointing
6. to arrive – career – to occur – interest – to embarrass
7. glass – success – buses – necessary – to disappear – embarrassing – grass
   possession – address – to disappoint – scissors
8. attempt – to attend – platform – committee

**b) Special consonants**
1. strength, bridge; 2. autumn, nephew, harbour, straight; 3. whether, wheel; 4. ghosts, whispered.

**s** *or* **c***?*
1. advice, practise; 2. advise, practice

**v** *or* **f***?*
1. lives, life; 2. believe, proof; 3. prove; 4. saved, safest, safe; 5. alive, saved; 6. live, Life

**Words, words, words.**
1. whether – straight – strength; 2. article – whistle – simple; 3. bridge – to exaggerate – judge; 4. character – practise – object; 5. harbour – government – ghost; 6. belief – to advise – autumn

### 3. Words with Special Vowels

15 **a) Special vowels**
1. marmalade – clerk – passage – to separate – assistant – passenger
2 apartment – human being – sergeant – engineer – queue – therefore – wherever – whenever – committee – madam – to rescue – pigeon – magazine – employee – café – medicine
3. bicycle – tobacco – parliament – thirst – balloon – brilliant – extraordinary – double – biscuit – juice – among – suburb – taxi

**b) One or two vowels?**
1. pronunciation, repeat; 2. explain, explanation; 3. pronounce, repeat, repetition

**c) ei** *or* **ie***?*
1. chief, receipt, received; 2. seized, thief; 3. niece; ceiling; 4. believe, deceiving

**d) Words, words, words**
1. suburb – thirst – queue; 2. among – double – tobacco; 3. parliament – taxi – bicycle; 4. apartment – medicine – visit; 5. pronunciation – explanation – repetition

### 4. Numerals and Other Words

15 **a) Numerals**
fourteen – five – eighty – twelve – fifteen – forty – eighteen – nine – four – fifty – eight
In the race, John came **ninth** out of **twelve**. Iqbal was **twelfth** and last.

**b) Words, words, words**
1. fifty – fifteen – twelve; 2. double – forty – fourteen; 3. nine – twelve – the ninth; 4. cannot – another – can't

**American Spelling**
color (A) – neighbour (B) – center (A) – license (A) – offence (B) – pretence (B) – traveled (A) – catalog (A) – programme (B) – check (A)

## B. Spelling of Inflected and Derived Forms

### 1. Final Silent -e

17

| | | | |
|---|---|---|---|
| 1. changing | insurance | noisy | noticeable |
| troublesome | paleness | queuing/queueing | seeing |
| noblest | completely | valuable | wholly |
| careful | arrival | noiseless | agreeable |
| moving | careless | ninety | changeable |
| movement | completing | ninth | truly |
| 2. writer | advertisement | moveable | amusement |
| shaving | advisable | pleasant | actively |
| hopeless | choosing | hopeful | lovely |
| refusal | pleasure | bluish | peaceful |
| sincerely | blameless | grateful | execution |
| believable | famous | assurance | managing |

3.

| | | | |
|---|---|---|---|
| usage | fortunately | gracious | arrangement |
| useful | imaginable | examination | icy |
| useable | pronounceable | manageable | noticing |
| useless | lonesome | replaceable | malicious |
| fortunate | adventurous | rescuing | serviceable |
| wholesome | graceful | behaviour | definable |

## 2. Final -y

17 a) y *or* i?

| | | | |
|---|---|---|---|
| carried | enjoying | marriage | annoying |
| carrying | happily | burial | furious |
| carriage | loneliness | glorious | emptiness |
| player | joyous | annoyance | buyer |
| playing | historical | penniless | enviable |
| easiness | prettily | trial | fiftieth |
| easiest | eightieth | merciful | buying |

b)
ladies – joys – essays – stories – boys – monkeys – copies – keys – valleys – berries – ways – companies – flies – chimneys – days – replies – enemies – cities – alleys

c)
tries – denies – prays – buries – annoys – says – worries – dries – dies – hurries – pays – fries – replies

d)
annoying, annoyed – hurrying, hurried – dying, died – drying, dried – tying, tied – playing, played – paying, paid – lying, lied – laying, laid – burying, buried – employing, employed – saying, said – buying, bought – qualifying, qualified – staying, stayed – obeying, obeyed – frying, fried – worrying, worried – praying, prayed

## 3. Final -o + s / 4. Final -f (-fe) + s

19 a)
potatoes – roofs – lives – thieves – shelves – scarves – tomatoes – calves – cliffs – chiefs – halves – pianos – wives – safes – selves – knives – handkerchiefs – leaves – studios – loaves – heroes – wolves

b)
1. wives, chiefs; 2. roofs, lives; 3. thieves, shelves; 4. potatoes, knives; 5. handkerchiefs, scarves; 6. themselves, heroes; 7. calves, wolves; 8. photos, cliffs

## 5. Doubling of Final Consonants

19

1. planned – beggar – hotter – wooden – coming – buses – stopping – thinnest – looking – robber – slipped – deeper – stepping – sunny – visitor – equipped – floating – developing – clapping – camping – cutting – shipping – humming – wettest – happening – sweater – profitable – becoming – dropping – beginner, flooded – swimming – brooding – profiting – happened – hoping, hopping – cleaning
2. stirred – colouring – barred – roaring – conference – cured – preferring – occurrence – prepared – differing – considered – boring – concurred – despaired – cleared – declared – abhorrence – covering – cheered

3. woollen – travelled – quarrelling – sailed – controller – peeled – traveller – quarrelled – shovelling – patrolled – cooler – tunnelled – available – controllable – boiled – compelled

### 6. Compound Words with -l

19 l *or* ll?
spoonful – farewell – always – all right – to fulfil – until – welcome – wonderful – skilful – almost – smallness – already – well-known – welfare – awful – till

## C. Special Problems

### 1. Capital Letters

21 a) About thirty people were present at my birthday party. Among them were Mum and Dad, Uncle Graham, Auntie Ellie, several cousins of mine and also some of my grandfather's friends, including Dr Robinson and Sir Alfred Garratt, his old professor.

b) Prince Charles is the successor to the Queen.

c) The northern part of Manhattan with Central Park is laid out like a chess board. The streets run east and west, the avenues north and south. The Rockefeller Center, a group of huge buildings, stretches from 48th to 51st Street. St Patrick's Cathedral, opposite the Rockefeller Center on Fifth Avenue, looks small among the skyscrapers. John F. Kennedy International Airport is one of the largest American airports.

d) The British Parliament consists of two houses, the House of Commons and the House of Lords. It sits on the banks of the river Thames. Tony Blair was Prime Minister from 1997–2007, when the Labour Party was the majority party in the House of Commons. In 2010, David Cameron became leader of a coalition between the Conservative Party and the Liberal Democrats.

e) The Sun is the biggest-selling daily paper in Britain, but The Times is the most famous.

f) A Tale of Two Cities / Alice in Wonderland / Harry Potter and the Goblet of Fire / The Scarlet Letter / The Old Man and the Sea / Lord of the Rings / The English School System / Radio, Television, the Press and the Internet / New Technology / A History of Computer Games / Britain in Europe

### 2. Some Abbreviations

21 1. 15,000 ft; 2. £10, £25; 3. 55 BC; 4. 8.30 a.m., 5.30 p.m.; 5. 5 ft, 6 in; 6. e.g.; 7. EU

# II. CHOICE OF WORDS

## A. Homophones, Homonyms, Homographs

### 1.1 Homophones

23 1. eye, I; 2. our, hour; 3. bye, by, buy; 4. break, brakes, break; 5. desert, dessert; 6. heir, air; 7. fair, fare, fair; 8. higher, hire; 9. here, hear; 10. hole, whole; 11. in, inn; 12. caught, court

**Just for Fun**
1. brakes; 2. whole, hole

### 1.2 Homophones

25 1. know, no; 2. knows, nose; 3. pain, pane; 4. piece, peace; 5. plain; plane; 6. right, write; 7. read, red; 8. rode, road; 9. sun, son; 10. sail, sale; 11. saw, sore; 12. stared, stairs; 13. two, too; 14. their, there; 15. threw, through; 16. one, won; 17. weigh, way; 18. wait, weight; 19. where, wear; 20. week, weak

### 2. Homonyms

27 1. cases; 2. bank; 3. match; 4. rest; 5. turkey; 6. desert; 7. bores; 8. lie

9. bank (= Bank / Sparkasse), bench (= Bank); 10. matches (= Streichhölzer), light (= anzünden); 11. light (= leicht); 12. ball (= (Ball); 13. ball (= Tanzveranstaltung); 14. race (= Rasse); 15. present (= Geschenk)

### 3. Homographs

27 1. tears; 2. tear; 3. desert; 4. live; 5. wind; 6. live

## B. Synonyms

### 1. old – aged – elderly – ancient – old-fashioned

29 a) old; b) aged; c) ancient; d) old; e) aged; f) old-fashioned

### 2. work – labour – task – job

a) work; b) task; c) labour; d) job, work; e) work; f) task

### 3. both – the two – either – neither

a) either; b) both; c) both; d) the two, both; e) neither; f) either

### 4. to visit – to go / to come to see – to attend / to go to

a) visit; b) attended; c) gone to; d) went to, visited; e) visit; f) visiting

### 5. ground – bottom – floor – land

a) floor; b) land; c) floor; d) ground; e) bottom; f) floor

### 6. to want – to need – to take – to use

31 a) takes; b) use; c) need; d) need; e) use; f) need / want, need / want

### 7. to bring – to fetch – to take – to carry – (to put)

a) take; b) take; c) bring; d) take; e) bring; f) take

### 8. to remind – to remember

a) remember; b) reminds; c) remember; d) remind; e) remember; f) remembers, remind

### 9. to excuse – to apologize – excuse me – sorry – pardon

a) excuse me; b) apologize; c) sorry; d) pardon; e) excuse me; f) sorry

### 10. to go – to travel – to run – to ride – to drive – to sail – to fly

33 a) travel / go; b) fly; c) drive; d) going; e) run; f) ride

### 11. colour – paint

a) paint; b) colour; c) colour-; d) paint; e) colours; f) paint

### 12. ready – finished – finish

a) finished; b) ready; c) finished, ready; d) ready; e) finish; f) ready

### 13.1 woman – wife – lady – madam – Mrs

a) madam; b) wife; c) woman; d) wife; e) wife; f) ladies

### 13.2 man – husband – gentlemen – sir – Mr

a) gentlemen; b) husband; c) man, Mr; d) husband; e) gentleman; f) sir

**Just for Fun**
Passenger: travelled / been; Taxi driver: driven

### 14. all – whole – complete – quite

35 a) complete; b) quite; c) all; d) whole; e) complete; f) quite

### 15. to go – to walk

a) walk; b) go; c) walk; d) walk; e) go; f) walk, go

### 16. happiness – luck – lucky

a) luck; b) happiness; c) lucky; d) luck; e) lucky; f) happiness

### 17. big – large – tall – great

a) big; b) tall; c) large / big, large / big; d) big; e) great; f) tall

### 18. to hold – to keep

a) keep; b) hold; c) holding; d) keep; e) keep; f) holding

Just for Fun
Mechanic to motorist: keep

### 19. to hear – to listen (to)

37 a) heard; b) listened; c) listen to; d) hear; e) hear; f) listened, hear, heard

### 20. each – every – any – either – anyone

a) each; b) either; c) anyone; d) any; e) any; f) every

### 21. small – little

a) little; b) small; c) little; d) little; e) small

### 22. to cook – to boil – to make

a) boil; b) make; c) cook; d) boiling; e) cooks; f) boiling, make

### 23. ill – sick

a) ill; b) sick; c) ill; d) sick; e) sick; f) sick

### 24. land – country

a) land; b) countries; c) country; d) land; e) land; f) country

### 25. to borrow – to lend – to hire

39 a) borrow; b) borrow, lend; c) hired; d) borrowed; e) lend; f) lend

### 26. to make – to do – (to take)

a) take; b) make; c) do; d) do, make; e) do; f) doing, making; g) take; h) take

### 27. to fit – to suit – to match

a) match; b) fit; c) suits; d) suit, fit; e) suit; f) fits, suit

### 28. price – prize

a) price; b) prize; c) prices; d) prize; e) price; f) price

### 29. journey – voyage – travel(s) – tour – trip

a) trip; b) travels; c) tour; d) journey; e) journey; f) tour

### 30. shade – shadow

a) shade; b) shadows; c) shade; d) shadow; e) shade; f) shadow

**Just for Fun**
Pupil: do

### 31. to say – to tell

41 a) told; b) said; c) say; d) said; e) tell; f) told

### 32. to seem – to shine

a) shining; b) seems; c) seems; d) shine; e) seem; f) seems

### 33. beautiful – handsome – pretty – fine – nice

a) beautiful; b) nice; c) fine; d) handsome; e) pretty; f) pretty

### 34. debt – fault – guilt

a) debts; b) guilt; c) fault; d) guilt; e) fault; f) debt

### 35.1 heavy – difficult – hard – serious (grave)

a) difficult; b) heavy; c) hard; d) hard / difficult; e) hard; f) grave

### 35.2 light – easy – slight

43 a) lighter; b) easy; c) slightly; d) easy; e) easy; f) easy

## 36. to see – to look – to stare – to glance

a) looking; b) staring; c) glanced; d) see; e) looks; f) stare

## 37. sure – certain – safe

a) safe; b) sure; c) certain; d) safe; e) certainly; f) safer

## 38. play – game – match

a) play; b) match; c) game; d) sport, matches; e) play; f) games

## 39. street – road – motorway

a) street; b) road; c) motorway; d) streets; e) road; f) motorway

**Just for fun**
Salesperson: light

## 40. to carry – to bear – to wear

45 a) bear; b) wearing; c) carry; d) bear; e) wear; f) wearing, carrying.

## 41. to differ / difference – to tell (apart)

a) differs; b) difference; c) tell; d) differ; e) difference; f) tell

## 42. to become – to get – to grow – to turn

a) getting; b) become; c) getting; d) became; e) getting, getting; f) turned, grew, got

## 43. to show – to point

a) pointed; b) showed; c) show; d) point; e) show; f) pointed

**Just for Fun**
Husband to wife: wearing

46 **Situational Practice**

**Are all the bosses stupid?**
*Lines:* 1. visiting; 2. land, work; 3. explained; 5. get; 7. job; 9. take; 11. both; 12. the two; 13. remember, needed; 14. get; 15. neither; 16. take, took; 17. remind; 18. used

**Mr Hall decorates the bathroom**
*Lines:* 1. Mrs, husband; 2. listen, keep; 3. Mrs, happy, heard; 4. paint; 5. drive, walk; 6. rode; 7. run over, whole; 8. luck, Mrs; 9. small, Mr, tall, each; 10. big, hold; 11. Mr, finished; 12. great, Mrs, colour; 13. anyone; 14. Mr, paint; 15. all, Mrs

47

**The strange guest**
*Lines:* 1. country, tour; 2. ill; 3. did, cook; 4. prize, lend; 5. went for, looked, said; 6. do; 7. price, making; 8. seems, said; 9. price

**Thick fog**
*Lines:* 1. see, tell; 2. safe, street; 3. got, sure

**Two different girls**
*Lines:* 1. match, difficult; 2. bear; 3. fault, pretty; 4. debts, beautiful; 6. easy, sure; 7. pretty, get; 8. heavy; 9. handsome, looked; 10. match, show

## C. Easily Confused Words

49

### 1. Nouns, Adjectives and Verbs

**1. bath – bathe**
a) bath; b) bathe, bathing; c) bathroom

**2. cloth – clothing, clothes**
a) clothes; b) cloth; c) clothes; d) clothing

**3. interested – interesting**
a) interesting; b) interested; c) interesting; d) interesting

**4. to arrive – to reach**
a) reached; b) arrived; c) arrived; d) reach

**5. to discover – to invent**
a) invented; b) discovered; c) discovered

**6. to notice – to realize – to remark**
a) noticed; b) realized; c) remarked; d) notice

**7. to overtake – to take over**
a) overtake; b) take over; c) overtook

**8. to own – to owe**
a) owes; b) owe; c) owns; d) owe

**9. past – passed**
a) passed; b) past; c) passed

**10. to rob – to steal**
a) stole; b) robbed; c) stolen; d) stole

**11. to take part – to take place**
a) take place; b) took part; c) take part; d) take place

**Just for Fun**
owes

### 2. A confusing verb

51 **12. to lie – to lay**
a) lies; b) laid; c) lay; d) lying; e) lie; f) lain

### 3. Adverbs

51 **13. first – at first**
a) first; b) at first; c) first; d) first; e) at first

**14. last – at last – at least**
a) at last; b) at least; c) last; d) at last; e) at least; f) at last

**15. sometimes – some time**
a) some time; b) sometimes; c) sometimes; d) some time; e) some time

**16. always – ever**
a) always; b) ever; c) always; d) ever; e) ever

## D. Misleading Words / False Friends

53 a)
1. bench; 2. get; 3. so; 4. poison; 5. possibly; 6. good; 7. corridor; 8. briefcase; 9. opinion; 10. murderer

11. topical; 12. perhaps; 13. grammar school; 14. humane; 15. make; 16. anxious; 17. kind; 18. university; 19. jam; 20. marks

55 b)
1. strict; 2. pension; 3. queue; 4. recipe; 5. donate

6. the next day; 7. prescription; 8. hiking; 9. saved; 10. die; 11. was surprised

**Situational Practice (Misleading Words)**

**Dreams**
*Lines:* 1. housemaster, Grammar School; 2. strict, opinion; 4. benches, corridors; 5. murderer, poison; 6. saved; 7. perhaps, get, pension; 8. bench, make; 9. the next day

**Just for Fun**
1. briefcase, floor, briefcase; 2. saved, saved

# E. Prepositions

## a. Nouns Preceded by Prepositions

### 1. Expressions of Place: at, in, on

57 **at, in** *or* **on?**

1. **on** a hill
2. **in** the country
3. **at** a party
4. **in** the kitchen
5. **on** the wall
6. **at** the butcher's
7. **in** Essex
8. **on** the Thames
9. **in** the picture
10. **on** the floor
11. **in** the world
12. **at** school
13. **in** the meeting
14. **in** the sky
15. **on** the coast
16. **in** Manchester
17. **at** the seaside
18. **in** the field
19. **at** the entrance
20. **on** the roof
21. **in** the sea
22. **at** the bus stop
23. **in** France
24. **at** lunch
25. **at** a short distance
26. **in** Oxford Street
27. **at** the bottom of the pool
28. **on** the corner of our street
29. **in** the corner of my room
30. **on** her way to school
31. **in** a small village
32. **on** the left-hand side
33. **at** the end of the queue
34. **in** the distance
35. **in** Trafalgar Square
36. **on** the road

1. **at** his desk
2. **in** the country
3. **at** the baker's
4. **on** the wall
5. **on** the roof
6. **at** the General Hospital
7. **in** Piccadilly Circus
8. **at** the top
9. **on** the lake
10. **in** the sky
11. **at** 10, Chapel Lane
12. **in** Oxford Street

1. on, at, on
2. at, at, on
3. on, on, in
4. in, at, in, in, in, on, at, in
5. on, at
6. in, in, in, in
7. at, in, in, at, at / in, in

### 2. Expressions of Time: at, in, on

59 a) **at, in** *or* **on?**

1. **at** noon
2. **on** Wednesday
3. **on** July 24th
4. **in** April
5. **at** that moment
6. **at** dinner time
7. **on** Christmas Day
8. **at** Easter
9. **in** Autumn
10. **at** night
11. **in** those days
12. **in** 2015
13. **at** twelve o'clock
14. **on** New Year's Day
15. **in** a few days
16. **on** my mother's birthday
17. **at** the age of 20
18. **at** half past six
19. **on** Monday
20. **in** the morning
21. **on** September 7th
22. **in** the night
23. **on** the morning of September 7th
24. **in** the afternoon

b)
1. **at** midday; 2. **in** the afternoon; 3. **at** noon; 4. **at** night; 5. **on** Sunday; 6. **at** the age of eighty; 7. **on** October 22nd; 8. **at** Easter; 9. **on** a fine day; 10. **on** time

c)
1. **in** the morning, **on** the morning of December 25th, **at** Christmas, **on** Christmas morning, **in** the evening of Christmas Day, **on** December 25th, **on** a Wednesday **in** December
2. **in** the end, **at** an end, **at** the end of the street
3. **at** night / **in** the afternoon / **at** sunset / **on** a sunny day / **in** the night / **at** six o'clock / **on** Thursday night / **at** noon / **in** the evening
4. **in** time, **at** the wrong time, **on** time

d)
1. at, in, on, at, in, at, in
2. on, at, in, on, at, in, on, in, on, in, on, in, at, at
3. on, in, at, in

### 3. Other Frequently Confused Prepositions

61 **after – behind**
1. after; 2. behind; 3. behind; 4. after

**ago – before**
1. ago; 2. ago; 3. ago, before; 4. ago; 5. before

**between – among**
1. between; 2. among; 3. between; 4. among; 5. between

**except – besides – beside**
1. except; 2. besides; 3. beside; 4. except; 5. besides; 6. besides

**for – since**
1. since; 2. since; 3. for; 4. for; 5. since; 6. for, since

**by – in – with**
1. in; 2. by, by; 3. with; 4. by; 5. with

**till / until – by**
1. by; 2. till; 3. by; 4. by; 5. till

**over – across – above – via / by**
1. across; 2. over; 3. across; 4. above / over; 5. over; 6. via

### 4. Nouns of Similar Meaning Preceded by the Same Preposition – by, for, in, *or* on ...

63 1. by; 2. in; 3. in; 4. for; 5. by, in; 6. for, in; 7. in; 8. by; 9. by, by; 10. on; 11. for; 12. on; 13. on; 14. by, for; 15. on

### 5. Some more prepositions

63 1. through; 2. during; 3. without; 4. after; 5. about; 6. towards

## b. Verbs and Adjectives Followed by Prepositions

### 1. Words Followed by Different Prepositions

65 **1. agree**
a) with; b) on; c) with, on; d) to; e) with

**2. angry (annoyed)**
a) about; b) with; c) with; d) about

**3. arrive**
a) in; b) at; c) at; d) at

**4. ask**
a) for; b) about; c) –; d) about; e) –

**5. call**
a) –; b) –; c) for; d) for; e) for, at

**6. care**
a) of; b) for; c) about; d) for; e) for

**7. consist / insist / persist**
a) on; b) of; c) of; d) on; e) in

**8. (in)dependent**
a) of; b) on; c) of; d) on

**9. hear**
a) of; b) from; c) about; d) from

**10. live**
a) with; b) on; c) on; d) at

67 **11. hope**
a) of; b) for; c) for; d) of

**12. look**
a) up; b) out; c) around; d) down on; e) after; f) forward to; g) up to; h) at

**13. speak**
a) about; b) up; c) to; d) about; e) to, about

**14. stay**
a) with; b) up; c) in; d) away

**15. take**
a) off; b) off

**16. think**
a) over; b) about; c) about

**17. write**
a) in, in; b) to; c) to; d) with

## 2. Words of Similar Meaning Followed by the Same Prepositions

69 **a) at – for – from?**
1. from; 2. for; 3. for; 4. at; 5. from; 6. for; 7. at; 8. for

**b) at – for – from – into?**
1. at; 2. from; 3. into; 4. for; 5. at; 6. at; 7. for; 8. from

**c) at – for – from – into?**
1. at; 2. into; 3. for; 4. for; 5. at; 6. at; 7. for; 8. at

71

**d) in – of – to?**
1. of; 2. in; 3. about; 4. of; 5. in; 6. in; 7. of; 8. to

**e) of – on – to – with?**
1. with; 2. on; 3. of; 4. with; 5. of; 6. on; 7. on; 8. with

**f) at – for – from – in – on – to – with?**
1. at, at; 2. to; 3. with; 4. to; 5. for; 6. to; 7. with; 8. on

72

**Situational Practice (Prepositions)**
1. *Lines:* 1. on, in, in, in; 2. of, by, in; 3. at, in; 4. at, on
2. *Lines:* 5. at; 6. at, in; 7. at, on, at; 8. to; 9. to; 10. on, in, by, on
3. *Lines:* 12. ago, in, with, to, for; 13. at, on

**Here is the News**
1. *Lines:* 1. at, in, in; 2. of, on; 3. for, of, by; 4. of
2. *Lines:* 5. for, at; 6. of, by, by, in; 7. at; 8. for, for
3. *Lines:* 9. on, on, near; 10. for, from; 11. in, out of, to; 12. from

**The Dog at the Cinema**
*Lines:* 1. at, on; 2. next to, at; 3. with, at, with; 4. with, at, to; 5. for, in; 6. with

73

**Big Steaks**
*Lines:* 1. on, in; 2. for, on, for, for; 3. at, at, of; 4. for, with; 5. with, for; 6. at, from, on

**Alison's New Job**
*Lines:* 1. in, for, at, of; 2. in, at; 3. of / about, at, about, of; 4. at, to; 5. for, of, on; 6. at, of, to; 7. in

**Just for Fun**
1. *Lines:* 1. on; 3. at, at; 4. For
2. *Lines*: 5. in, for, in; 6. until, at
3. *Lines*: 7. to; 9. from; 11. on

# III. GRAMMAR

## A. Nouns

### 1. The Formation of the Plural

75

| | | | | |
|---|---|---|---|---|
| 1. stories | children | buses | potatoes | women |
| monkeys | wishes | roofs | boxes | matches |
| feet | knives | men | photos | ladies |
| safes | kilos | thieves | mice | geese |

| | | | | |
|---|---|---|---|---|
| 2. people | flies | journeys | leaves | halves |
| tomatoes | heroes | lives | pianos | wives |
| essays | radios | cherries | cliffs | ponies |
| classes | wolves | months | copies | donkeys |
| holidays | bridges | plays | loaves | lorries |
| noises | families | parties | countries | cities |

### 2. The Use of Singular and Plural

75 **a) English: Plural – German: Singular (Parts of the Body and Articles of Clothing)**
1. The ladies **kept their hats** on.
2. They shook **their heads** in disbelief.
3. The boys were standing there with **their hands in their pockets.**
4. The demonstrators turned **their backs** on the policemen.
5. The rescuers risked **their lives** to save the mountaineers.

**b) million, thousand, etc.**
1. I bought two **dozen** eggs for the cake.
2. **Thousands** of workers were on strike.
3. The bridge will cost 10 **million** dollars.
4. This project will cost **millions** of dollars.
5. Two **hundred** passengers were on board the ship when it sank.
6. Two **million** five **hundred thousand** pounds were stolen.

77 **c) Only in the Singular**
1. piece of news; 2. furniture; 3. information; 4. progress; 5. piece of advice; 6. knowledge; 7. news; 8. furniture

**d) Only in the Plural**
1. trousers; 2. a pair of scissors; 3. pyjamas; 4. glasses; 5. pair of glasses; 6. pairs of shorts, pants; 7. jeans; 8. pairs of jeans; 9. wages

**e) Concord**
1. Where **are the scissors**?
2. Here **is** the 10 o'clock **news.**
3. Where **are** my brown **trousers**?
4. **The furniture** in this room **is** from IKEA.
5. **The information** I got **was** not very useful.
6. **The stairs are** not easy to climb.
7. My wages **are** better than they were last year.
8. His advice **has** not always been good.
9. Bad news **travels** fast.
10. **These are** my father's glasses.
11. The United States **is** a world power.
12. Physics **is** an important subject.

### 3. Genitive

79

**a) The Form of the s-Genitive**
1. my brother's bike; 2. the children's toys; 3. a woman's dress; 4. the soldiers' uniforms; 5. Dickens's books; 6. my sister's car; 7. Mr Jones's garden; 8. women's rights; 9. my parents' car; 10. the child's bed

**b) 'of' or s-Genitive?**
1. the politician's speech; 2. the author of that book; 3. the baker's; 4. the windows of the house; 5. yesterday's newspaper; 6. Mr Burns's car; 7. at my aunt's; 8. our neighbours' dog

**c) The of-Attribute**
1. the month of August; 2. two bottles of milk and two kilos of potatoes; 3. the river Nile; 4. the Houses of Parliament, the City of London; 5. in the year 2012, near Lake Windermere; 6. at the University of California

**Situational Practice (Nouns)**

**Moving Day**
*Lines:* 1. their heads, piece of news; 2. children, made up their minds / decided, the River Avon; 3. city of Coventry, fifteen year-old; 4. twenty-pound note, four hours'; 5. stories, dozen; 6. my aunt's head, furniture was; 7. stairs, contents of the chest, trousers, pairs of jeans, pair of pyjamas, hundreds of, my uncle's; 8. possessions, of the house, knives; 9. pair of scissors, hours', a cup of tea; 10. wages

## B. Articles

### 1. The Definite Article

81

**a) Names**
1. –, the Charlie Holt who; 2. in the summer of 2012, in the Canaries; 3. –; 4. –, –; 5. near the Tower, –, –; 6. the Sunday, the Thames, –; 7. the Smiths, in the afternoon; 8. the United Kingdom, –; 9. –; 10. the Danube, in the Black Forest, into the Black Sea; 11. –, the Queen's residence; 12. in the Lake District, –, –

**b) Names of Species, Materials, Abstract Nouns, etc.**
1. –; 2. –, the milk; 3. the strong, the weak; 4. –; 5. –; 6. –, –; 7. –, –, –; 8. the time, the best time; 9. –, the school; 10. –

### 2. The Indefinite Article

83

**a) Use of the Indefinite Article**
1. –; 2. what a stupid thing; 3. –; 4. –; 5. –; 6. –; 7. as a boy, a pilot; 8. –; 9. a birthday present; 10. it's a pity, a headache

**b) Position of Articles**
1. **half an** hour later; 2. it is **too** hot **a** day; 3. **quite a** lot of people; 4. **rather a** bad cold; 5. **such** long hair

6. **all the** houses; 7. **half the** cake; 8. in **all** directions; 9. **all the** windows; 10. **both** sisters

**Situational Practice (Articles)**

**A Visit to London**
1. *Lines:* 1. around **the** city, from Trafalgar Square; 2. to Hyde Park, from Buckingham Palace, to **the** London Eye, in **the** summer; 3. the banks of **the** Thames, in **an** open-topped bus, in **a** hurry; 4. by underground, time, life, in half, **the** time; 5. Transport For London

2. *Lines:* 6. by most of **the** Germans, visited **the** school; 7. **a** teacher, quite **a** large school, in **the** United Kingdom, all **the** boys and girls; 8. to school, in **the** mornings, had dinner; 9. time, most, through Southern England; 10. **the** time we spent in London, what weather, summer; 11. **a** cough, **a** pity, most people, such **a** visit; 12. **a** good thing

## C. Pronouns

### 1. Personal Pronouns

85 **a) Forms of the 3rd Person**
1. they, them; 2. she, her; 3. it, it; 4. she, her; 5. it, it

**b) 'He, she, it, they' and 'there' for German 'es'**
1. it's; 2. there was; 3. there was; 4. it's; 5. it was, she's; 6. there is; 7. it was; 8. they are; 9. is there; 10. there were

**c) Other Equivalents for German 'es'**
1. so; 2. –; 3. so; 4. –, –; 5. so; 6. –; 7. so; 8. –; 9. so; 10. –;

### 2. Reflexive and Reciprocal Pronouns

87 **a) Emphasizing Pronouns**
1. themselves; 2. himself; 3. yourself; 4. myself; 5. yourself; 6. himself

**b) Reflexive Pronouns**
1. him; 2. herself; 3. us; 4. himself; 5. her; 6. herself

c)
1. each other; 2. themselves; 3. each other; 4. each other; 5. themselves; 6. yourself

### 3. Possessive Pronouns

87 **a) Possessive Adjective or Definite Article?**
1. your, your; 2. the; 3. his; 4. the; 5. my; 6. his; 7. the; 8. their; 9. her, her; 10. its

**b) The Possessive Adjective with 'own'**
1. in his own aeroplane; 2. a car of his own; 3. my own eyes; 4. your own toothbrush; 5. a bike of my own; 6. their own house

**c) Possessive Pronouns**
1. theirs, yours, hers; 2. yours, mine; 3. yours; 4. his; 5. theirs

## 4. Demonstrative Pronouns

89

**a) Forms and Use**
1. this is, this; 2. these, those ones; 3. those were; 4. these are, those are; 5. these are; 6. are these

**b) The Propword 'one'**
1. this one; 2. these ones or those ones; 3. this one or that one; 4. those, these ones; 5. this one or that one; 7. this, that one.

## 5. Interrogative Pronouns

89

**a) who, whose – what?**
1. who; 2. what; 3. who; 4. whose; 5. who; 6. what; 7. who; 8. what

9. what; 10. who; 11. who; 12. whose; 13. who; 14. what; 15. who; 16. who; 17. who; 18. what

**b) which – what?**
1. which; 2. what; 3. what; 4. which; 5. what; 6. what; 7. which; 8. which

9. which; 10. what (kind of); 11. what; 12. which; 13. which; 14. which; 15. what; 16. which

## 6. Relative Pronouns

91

**a) Defining and Non-Defining Relative Clauses**
1. This house, which was built in 1870, will soon be demolished.
2. The house which is going to be demolished was built in 1870.
3. The man you met last night is my partner.
4. Oliver, who you met last night, is my partner.
5. Richard, whose friends live in England, speaks English very well.
6. The man whose name is best known in America is probably Barack Obama.

**b) Defining Relative Clauses**
1. which; 2. who; 3. –; 4. –; 5. which; 6. –; 7. –; 8. –

**c) who, whose, whom, which, that, what *or* nothing?**
1. She had a list of things she wanted to buy.
2. Shakespeare, whose father was a butcher, was the greatest English dramatist.
3. Nick is just the person we need for the job.
4. Cricket is a game I absolutely love.
5. Is there a shop **which** sells SIM cards near here?
6. My aunt Dorothy, **who** you know quite well, is seriously ill.
7. He regrets **what** he has done.
8. Lake Windermere, **which** is 10 miles long, is the longest lake in England.

## 7. Indefinite Pronouns

93

**a) much, many – little, few**
1. many; 2. much; 3. much; 4. much; 5. many; 6. many

7. few; 8. many; 9. few; 10. a little; 11. few; 12. a little

**b) "some" and "any" and their compounds**
1. any, some; 2. some, any; 3. any, any, some; 4. any; 5. some; 6. any

7. any, someone; 8. someone, anything; 9. something, any; 10. something, anyone; 11. some, anything; 12. some, any; 13. anyone; 14. something

**c) nobody, nothing – none, neither**
1. nobody; 2. neither; 3. nothing; 4. none; 5. neither; 6. nobody

**Situational Practice (Pronouns)**
there are, lots of, of mine, who, his own hotel, a few
1. Customer: something which, which, these, this one; Waiter: so; Customer: what
2. Customer: your, myself; Waiter: it

# D. Adjectives and Adverbs

## 1. Comparison

95 **a)**
simple – simpler – simplest
skilled – more skilled – most skilled
easy – easier – easiest
famous – more famous – most famous
many – more – most
little – less – least
quickly – more quickly – most quickly
good – better – best
bad – worse – worst
deep – deeper – deepest
noble – nobler – noblest
carefully – more carefully – most carefully
narrow – narrower – narrowest
perfect – more perfect – most perfect
early – earlier – earliest
excited – more excited – most excited
new – newer – newest
badly – worse – worst
few – fewer – fewest
difficult – more difficult – most difficult
usual – more usual – most usual
sincere – more sincere – most sincere
gentle – gentler – gentlest
thin – thinner – thinnest
fast – faster – fastest
probably – more probably – most probably
pleased – more pleased – most pleased
long – longer – longest
useful – more useful – most useful
lovely – lovelier – loveliest
frequently – more frequently – most frequently
clever – cleverer – cleverest
tall – taller – tallest
hot – hotter – hottest
interesting – more interesting – most interesting
big – bigger – biggest
terrible – more terrible – most terrible
independent – more independent – most independent
slowly – more slowly – most slowly
heavy – heavier – heaviest
beautiful – more beautiful – most beautiful
easily – more easily – most easily
much – more – most
soon – sooner – soonest

**b) little, few, bad**, etc.
1. less; 2. fewest; 3. less; 4. worse; 5. best, worst.

**c) nearest** *or* **next, latest** *or* **last?**
1. nearest; 2. next; 3. next; 4. latest, last; 5. last; 6. latest

**d) German 'immer'**
1. Fewer and fewer; 2. worse and worse; 3. again and again

**e) Comparison in the sentence**
1. than, as ... as; 2. as ... as, than; 3. than, as ... as; 4. as ... as, than; 5. worse than

## 2. Adjectives Used as Nouns

95 a)
1. old, sick; 2. old people; 3. blind; 4. blind people; 5. English, English people

b)
1. the rich, poor people; 2. the French

## 3. Adjectives with Propword (one / ones)

97 1. one, one; 2. –; 3. –, –, –; 4. one; 5. –; 6. –

## 4. Adjectives or Adverbs?

97 1. easy, useful, easily, correct; 2. really, surprising, careless, carefully; 3. generally, occasionally, unusual; 4. bad, slowly, surprisingly, quick; 5. quickly, good; 6. terribly, hot, fresh, good; 7. excitedly, angry; 8. delicious, awful.

## 5. Peculiarities of Adjectives and Adverbs

97 1. hardly; 2. hard; 3. hard, hardly; 4. lately; 5. late; 6. fairly; 7. fair; 8. pretty

## 6. English Verbs instead of German Adverbs

99 1. happened to see him; 2. I hope / hopefully; 3. unfortunately; 4. prefer; 5. went on playing; 6. seems to be

## 7. The Position of Adverbs

99

1. They are going to London **tomorrow**.
2. Auntie Jane stayed **with us in October**.
3. I saw her **on the bus last night.**
4. I've **never** heard such nonsense.
5. He was **badly** hurt in an accident.
6. Have you **ever** eaten oysters?
7. I had **completely** forgotten the meeting.
8. Pete is **always** thirsty.
9. I'm **usually** home **by five o'clock**.
10. We are going **abroad this year**.

**Situational Practice (Adjectives and Adverbs)**

**Mars, Saturn or the Sun?**
*Lines:* 2. one; 3. happened to meet, early; 4. Englishman, bigger than; 6. as ... as, most interesting; 8. hard, bigger, better, unfortunately; 9. probable, unhappy; 10. latest; 11. pretty, on Saturn next week; 12. suddenly, sadder and sadder, best; 13. excitedly; 14. terribly hot; 15. as ... as

**Just for Fun**
Diner: strange, carefully

# E. Auxiliary Verbs

## 1. Questions and Negatives

101

**a) Questions**
**1. Yes / No Questions**
1. Does your dad work hard? 2. Do their friends live in London? 3. Did he go to the cinema at the weekend? 4. Does Chris drink a pint of beer after dinner? 5. Did they go to the cinema? 6. Must he go now? 7. Did he do his homework in the evening? 8. Can the students understand what the teacher says? 9. Will they arrive at six o'clock? 10. Were there were a lot of people at the meeting? 11. Are the boys playing football? 12. Does the bus stop here?

**2. Questions with 'who, whose, which, what, where, when, how'**
1. Who lives in Coventry? 2. Where does your father's friend live? 3. Whose friend lives in Coventry? 4. When do they get up? 5. Who met his friend at the station? 6. Who did Tim meet at the station? 7. Where did Tim meet his friend? 8. Where is Tim going to meet his friend? 9. Who has been in Edinburgh since Easter. 10. Where has your sister been since Easter? 11. Who cleaned the kitchen yesterday? 12. What did Richard clean yesterday?

**b) Negative Sentences**
1. They didn't go to the cinema. 2. Don't be an idiot! 3. I hope not. 4. He didn't ask for help. 5. Don't be so shy! 6. Don't come between one and three p.m.

**Just For Fun**
"Why **can't** you make up your mind? On your thirtieth birthday you cried because you **didn't want** to be thirty, and now you're crying because you **do** want to be thirty."

103

**c) Questions and Negatives with 'have'**

| | | |
|---|---|---|
| 1. | a) don't have; | b) Do they have ...? |
| 2. | a) hasn't got; | b) Has he got ...? |
| 3. | a) didn't have; | b) Did they have ...? |
| 4. | a) hasn't done; | b) Has he done ...? |
| 5. | a) doesn't have to get up; | b) Does Alan have to get up ...? |
| 6. | a) didn't have; | b) Did Mrs Lee have ...? |
| 7. | a) didn't have; | b) Did she have ...? |
| 8. | a) don't have; | b) Do the Smiths have ...? |
| 9. | a) hasn't read; | b) Has your father read ...? |
| 10. | a) didn't have a party last night; | b) Did your friends have ...? |

## 2. Auxiliaries in Short Sentences and Question Tags

103

**a) Short Answers**
1. Yes, he is. No, he isn't. 2. Yes, I have. No, I haven't. 3. Yes, I did. No, I didn't. 4. Yes, he does. No, he doesn't. 5. Yes, he has. No, he hasn't. 6. Yes, she can. No, she can't. 7. Yes, they were. No, they weren't. 8. Yes, she is. No, she isn't.

**b) Short Sentences**
1. So do I. 2. Nor can his sister. 3. Nor do I. 4. So does Will. 5. So can Tom. 6. So did Karen. 7. So do I. 8. So must I.

**c) Question Tags**
1. isn't she? 2. did you? 3. won't she? 4. isn't it? 5. haven't you? 6. isn't he? 7. will he? 8. didn't you?

### 3. Defective Auxiliaries

105

**a) Ability**
1. can; 2. was able to; 3. was able to; 4. will be able to; 5. wasn't able to, will be able to; 6. would have been able to; 7. can; 8. was able to

9. könntest du?; 10. konnten nicht; 11. könnten; 12. hätte kommen können

**b) Possibility**
1. must; 2. would; 3. must; 4. may; 5. might; 6. might

**c) Permission**
1. May / Can, may / can, may not / can't; 2. aren't allowed to; 3. were allowed to;
4. May / Can, may not / can't; 5. aren't allowed to; 6. mustn't

107

**d) Obligation, Necessity**
1. must; 2. has to; 3. do you have to; 4. has to; 5. must; 6. had to

**Absence of Obligation and Necessity: don't have to – need not**
1. don't have to; 2. didn't have to; 3. don't have to; 4. didn't have to

**Prohibition or Absence of Obligation: mustn't – don't need to**
1. don't need to; 2. don't need to; 3. doesn't need to; 4. don't need to; 5. mustn't

**e) 'sollen'**
1. should; 2. should; 3. should; 4. should; 5. should / ought to; 6. shouldn't have made

**f) 'wollen'**
1. wants to; 2. wanted to, wouldn't; 3. want to; 4. wanted to; 5. wanted to; 6. would; 7. want to

**Situational Practice (Auxiliary Verbs)**
1. *Lines:* 1. had to; 2. must have got out; 3. wanted to, didn't have, may; 4. didn't you, did you do; 5. can, could, don't want to
2. *Lines:* 6. haven't I, you shouldn't, have got, haven't you; 7. don't fight, shouldn't have believed you

## F. Continuous Form and Simple Form

109

**a) Present Tense**
1. is raining; 2. is doing; 3. am washing; 4. plays; 5. is Dad doing, is watching; 6. do you get, go by bus, walk; 7. is boiling; 8. is coming; 9. are you waiting, am waiting; 10. is playing, plays

**b) Past Tense**
1. was swimming; 2. played; 3. arrived, were sitting; 4. were you doing, was watching; 5. watched; 6. was crossing; 7. did you play; 8. broke, was eating; 9. left, was raining; 10. was eating, rang

111

**c) Verbs not used in the Continuous Form / Series of Actions**
**1. Present tense**: a) see; b) tastes; c) seems; d) does your father own; e) what does … contain; f) hates
**Past tense:** g) wanted; h) left, switched; i) crossed, went, sat

**2.**
a) was reading, went; b) think, is playing, likes; c) were you walking, saw; d) smiled, saw; e) do you know, think, met; f) broke, heard; g) don't know, belong; h) arrived, was working, was washing, were watching

**Situational Practice (Continuous Form and Simple Form)**
1. *Lines:* 1. visited, lived, was walking, noticed; 2. owned, was barking, does ... bark; 3. looked, thought, tasted; 4. replied, always barks, barks; 5. bites; 6. was watching, speaking, know; 7. know, knows
2. *Lines:* 8. were walking, they were doing; 9. are carrying
3. *Lines:* 12. know, stands, watches; 14. knows; 15. thought

**Just for Fun**
1. are you doing; fell; am trying
2. are you doing; am helping

## G. The Use of Tenses

### 1. Past Tense and Present Perfect

113

**a) Past Tense or Present Perfect?**
1. finished; 2. did you meet; 3. have you seen; 4. was, lived; 5. have just finished; 6. have never eaten; 7. did you sleep; 8. have already had; 9. hasn't finished, yet; 10. did you buy; 11. hasn't arrived yet; 12. did you do

**b) Past Tense or Present Perfect?**
1. went, has been; 2. has she been; 4. broke, hasn't been able; 5. had, haven't had; 6. did you have, haven't had

**Present Perfect Simple or Continuous?**
1. have you been learning; 2. have been waiting; 3. have only heard; 4. has been sitting; 5. has not seen; 6. has been raining; 7. have lived; 8. have known

**c) Past Tense or Present Perfect (Simple or Continuous)?**
1. have been waiting, waited; 2. has not seen, moved, has he lived; 3. have lost, have you seen, saw; 4. was, met, have you been; 5. has had, was, bought, had, has had; 6. studied, started, has been studying

### 2. Past Tense and Past Perfect

115

**Past Tense or Past Perfect (Simple or Continuous)?**
1. returned, had already begun; 2. had been waiting, came; 3. told, had helped; 4. had read, rang; 5. had been learning, went; 6. came, had left; 7. had known, came; 8. was, had been

### 3. Forms of the Future

115

**a) will-Future or Present Tense?**
1. will be; 2. will stay, get; 3. will catch; 4. will arrive soon; 5. will you do, doesn't come; 6. will be; 7. will arrive; 8. will be, sees; 9. will help, ask; 10. is, will have

**b) will-Future or 'going to'?**
1. am going to have; 2. are you going to eat; 3. will be; 4. are you going to do; 5. will work; 6. is going to wash; 7. will you write; 8. will fail

**c) will-Future or Present Continuous?**
1. are playing; 2. am going, are you coming; 3. will know; 4. are staying; 5. am having; 6. won't cost; 7. will break; 8. are getting

**d) Future Continuous or Future Perfect?**
1. will be waiting; 2. will have cooked; 3. will be arriving; 4. will have finished; 5. will be doing; 6. will have been

## 4. Reported Speech

117 **a) The Use of Tenses in Reported Speech (Statements)**
1. He says **he wants to go home.** 2. He said **he wanted to go home.** 3. He said **he would go at once.** 4. The young man said that **he could speak four languages.** 5. Mrs Drummond replied that **I could use her phone.** 6. Mrs Drummond said that **Mike could use her phone.** 7. Sue says **she doesn't like cauliflower.** 8. The girls keep shouting that **their team will win.** 9. The girls shouted that **their team would win.** 10. The notice says that **no dogs are allowed in the park.**

**b) Questions**
1. My friend asked me **when I was going to the football match.** 2. He wanted to know **if / whether I was going to the football match.** 3. He asked **if / whether I often played football.** 4. He wants to know **where my brother Tom is.** 5. Can you tell me **if / whether the boys are playing in the garden?** 6. Emily asked Harriet **whether she was interested in the environment.** 7. The man asked me **what the time was.** 8. She asked me **if / whether I had ever taken drugs.** 9. Do you know **if / whether the postman has been here?**

119 **c) Commands and Requests**
1. *Mr Roberts* told **me to take a message to the headteacher.** 2. *Mr Roberts* told **Sue to take a message to the headteacher.** 3. My aunt asked **me not to play football in the garden.** 4. My father warned **me not to swim out too far.** 5. Jane asked **Gary to help her find the key.** 6. The teacher told **us not to make so much noise.** 7. The girl next to me at the table asked **me to pass her the salt.** 8. Mrs Todd invited **her guests to have a cup of tea.** 9. The owner told **us not to smoke in that room.** 10. Mrs Hill told her children **to brush their teeth and go to bed.**

**d) Changes of Demonstratives and Adverbs in Reported Statements, Questions and Commands**
1. Jack said **he was going to see his friends in Coventry the next day.** 2. The author's wife said **that he had written that novel a long time before.** 3. Ben wanted to know **how many lessons I had had the week before.** 4. John said **he couldn't come that day.** 5. Mr Bowen added **that he had been in London the week before.** 6. Rosie asked Maggie **where she had been the night before.**

## 5. Conditional Clauses

121 **a) Type 1: Conditional I**
1. We **will go** for a walk if the weather **is** nice. 2. If you **don't hurry**, you **will miss** the train. 3. If he **asks** me, I **will help** him. 4. If you **go**, I **will come** with you. 5. You **will get** home earlier if you **walk** faster. 6. If you **ring** the bell, they **will let** you in. 7. We **can go** by bus if we **miss** the train. 8. If you **drop** your phone, it **will break.**

**b) Type II: Improbable Condition / Unreal Present / Conditional II**
1. He **could** work much harder if he **tried.** 2. She **would come** if she **had** time. 3. If I **found** a ten-pound note, I **would take** it to the police. 4. If he **didn't love** her, he **wouldn't marry** her. 5. I **wouldn't do** it if I **didn't like** it. 6. Adam **wouldn't be** so fat if he **ate** less. 7. What **would you do** with her if she **was** your daughter? 8. If I **won** the lottery, I **would travel** round the world.

**c) Type III: Impossible Condition / Unreal Past**
1. We **wouldn't have gone** to the party if we **hadn't been** invited. 2. If she **had taken** her umbrella, she **wouldn't have got** wet. 3. She **would have stayed** in her job if the pay **had been** better. 4. I **wouldn't have made** a mistake if I **had known** that. 5. If we **hadn't drunk** so much, we **wouldn't have got** a headache. 6. If Mark **hadn't said** anything, nobody **would have known** about it. 7. He **would have caught** the train if he **had left** earlier. 8. I **would have bought** the shirt if it **hadn't been** so expensive.

**d) Types I, II, III Mixed**
1. If I get the money, I will buy a new bike. If I got the money, I would buy a new bike. If I had got the money, I would have bought a new bike.
2. If we go by train, we will arrive earlier. If we went by train, we would arrive earlier. If we had gone by train, we would have arrived earlier.
3. He will lend you the money if you ask him. He would lend you the money if you asked him. He would have lent you the money if you had asked him.
4. If he has time, he will go to the cinema. If he had time, he would go to the cinema. If he had had time, he would have gone to the cinema.

5. starts; 6. would have taken; 7. lent; 8. wouldn't swim; 9. would you do; 10. leave; 11. drank; 12. were

**Situational Practice (Tenses)**
1. *Lines:* 1. was, have believed; 2. possessed, would give; 3. owned, would let; 4. had, would you give

2. *Lines:* 7. wrote, was, worked, had finished; 8. decided, wanted, will become; 9. have published, have lived; 10. have always been, have been writing, will still be writing, am

*Reported speech:* Robert said that he **had written** his first book when he **was** twenty. Before that he had **worked** for four years on 'The Times'. After he **had finished** his university studies, he **decided** that all he **wanted** to do was write, so he said to himself that one day he **would become** a successful author." Since then he **had published** over thirty books. He **had lived** in England for most of his life, and he **had always been** very happy. He **had been writing** novels for fifty years, and he hoped he **would still be writing** when he **was** ninety.

3. *Lines:* 12. had never spoken; 14. haven't you ever said, has been

## H. The Non-Finite Forms of Full Verbs: -ing Form (Gerund and Participle)

123 **a) The *-ing* Form (Gerund) as a Subject and after Certain Expressions**
1. The museum is worth looking round. 2. It's no use waiting for a taxi here. 3. It's not worth going to that film.

4. These boots aren't worth mending. 5. I don't feel like going for a walk. 6. He is busy working in his office. 7. It was worth coming to the gig. 8. I don't feel like swimming now.

**b) The *-ing* Form (Gerund) as an Object**
1. cooking; 2. making; 3. opening; 4. doing; 5. smoking; 6. playing

**c) The *-ing* Form (Gerund) after Prepositions**
1. studying; 2. seeing; 3. telling; 4. going; 5. visiting

6. driving; 7. play; 8. smoke; 9. having; 10. reading

# I. The Use of Certain Conjunctions, Adverbs and Prepositions

125

**a) German 'auch (nicht)'**
1. too; 2. so; 3. also; 4. either; 5. neither / nor; 6. too; 7. as well; 8. neither

9. as well; 10. too; 11. as well

12. She **doesn't** speak Italian **either**. 13. He **doesn't** play golf, and he **doesn't** play tennis **either**.
14. Nina **doesn't like** skiing, and she **doesn't like** skating **either**.

**b) German 'wenn'**
1. if; 2. when; 3. when; 4. when; 5. if; 6. when; 7. if; 8. when

**c) German 'während'**
1. during; 2. while; 3. while; 4. whereas; 5. while; 6. during; 7. while; 8. during

**d) German 'da, weil'**
1. because; 2. as; 3. because; 4. as; 5. as; 6. because

**e) German 'wie'**
1. like; 2. as … as; 3. as; 4. as … as; 5. like; 6. as … as; 7. as … as; 8. like

**Just for Fun (Conjunctions, etc.)**
1. "If I had a kid like yours, I wouldn't hurry home either."
2. while, as, during
3. because, when, whereas, when

# IV. PRONUNCIATION

## A. Word Stress

### 1. Words of Two Syllables

127 1. Ju**ly**; 2. eff**e**ct; 3. addr**e**ss; 4. compl**e**te; 5. **e**ffort; 6. c**o**ncert; 7. pol**i**ce; 8. d**i**strict; 9. can**a**l; 10. m**e**dicine; 11. succ**e**ss; 12. acc**ou**nt; 13. extr**e**me; 14. hot**e**l

**Situational Practice**
1. **pur**pose, **pur**chase, **cos**tume, **the**atre, on**line**
2. **as**pects, **de**tail, **pro**gramme, **A**pril
3. ad**vis**ed, com**plete**, **me**dicine, **or**anges, **sa**lad
4. Ju**ly**, **Au**gust, can**oe**, can**a**ls, can**oe**, **ba**lance, **sur**face

**The Tramp**
*Lines:* 1. **sea**son; 2. hot**el**, pol**ice**; 3. **sig**nal; 4. **coll**eagues, **se**cret; 5. **or**gan; 6. **com**fort, compl**ete**, **eff**ort; 7. al**though**, **fut**ure, **brill**iant; 8. car**ee**r, **art**ist, **pil**ot, **priv**ate, acc**ount**, **ga**rage; 9. **fig**ure, po**lice**man; 10. con**cern**; 11. po**lice**man

### 2. Words of Three and More Syllables

129 1. therm**o**meter; 2. distr**i**bute, 3. democr**a**tic; 4. elem**e**ntary; 5. **e**xercise; 6. n**e**gative; 7. engin**ee**r; 8. parliam**e**ntary; 9. spect**a**tor; 10. repres**e**ntative; 11. id**e**a; 12. to introd**u**ce; 13. cert**i**ficate; 14. cigar**e**tte

**Situational Practice**
1. ther**mom**eter, **in**strument, **hos**pitals, **al**ready, dis**trib**uted
2. **con**ference, **ev**ident, **pres**ident's, **att**itude, **min**ister's, id**eas**, en**tire**ly, **neg**ative, **In**ternet, **in**terview, de**ter**mined, ex**am**ine
3. **al**phabet, **con**sonants, **dic**tionary, **al**phabet, **ar**ticle, in**fin**itive, **rel**ative, sup**er**lative

**The Troubles in Northern Ireland**
*Lines:* 1. **Cath**olics; 2. **priv**ileges, **Prot**estant, **nec**essary; 3. **Prot**estant, **Cath**olics; 4. **pol**itics, **Prot**estants; 5. **el**ements, parlia**ment**ary, de**moc**racy; 6. democr**at**ic, **Cath**olics; 7. repre**sent**atives, **Parl**iament, **Prot**estants, Con**serv**ative, **Min**ister; 9. **com**promise, **Min**ister, **Sec**retary

### 3. Different Stress in Homographs

131 1. des**ert**ed, **des**ert; 2. **sub**ject, **de**crease, **im**ports; 3. **pro**gress, pro**gress**ing, per**fect**; 4. con**duct**ed, **rec**ord; 5. **pres**ent **per**fect, **pres**ent; 6. prot**ests**, ob**ject**, **in**crease

### 4. Different Stress in Cognate Words

1. In**dus**trial, **ec**onomic ad**vant**age, com**par**ed, **in**dustry, ec**on**omy
2. **com**parable, po**lit**ical, com**par**atively; 3. **dem**onstrate, demon**strat**ions

### 5. Level Stress (Double Stress)

1. H**y**de P**a**rk, H**y**de Park C**o**rner; 2. f**i**rst-class r**e**staurant, l**oo**ks first-cl**a**ss; 3. N**o**rth S**ea**, but N**o**rth Sea **oi**l; 4. s**e**venteen g**i**rls, th**i**rt**ee**n; 5. s**e**cond-hand b**oo**ks, s**e**cond-h**a**nd; 6. out**doors**, **ou**tdoor g**a**mes

# B. Sounds and Their Spelling

## 1. Vowels and Diphthongs

133 **a**

1. passport /ɑː/; 2. bare /eə/; 3. grand /æ/; 4. straight /eɪ/; 5. danger /eɪ/; 6. he said /e/; 7. alphabet /æ/; 8. purchase /ə/; 9. cause /ɔː/; 10. I say /eɪ/; 11. wallet /ɒ/; 12. sausage /ɒ/; 13. chance /ɑː/; 14. because /ɒ/

**Situational Practice**
1. /ˈmɑːsɪz/, /strɔː/, /ˈplæstɪk/, /gæs/ /mɑːsks/, /feɪntɪd/, /bɪˈkɒz/, /kɔːz/
2. /ɑːnt/, /sed/, /ˈdɔːtə/, /əˈfreɪd/, /kɑːnt/, /sɔːlt/, /ˈsɒsɪdʒɪz/, /ˈkwɒləti/, /ˈbrekfəst/, /ˈdɒləz/, /tʃeɪndʒ/
3. /lɔː/, /dʒeɪl/, /ˈmeni/, /rɪˈwɔːd/
4. /ˈveɪkənt/, /ˈæŋgri/, /fɔːlt/, /sed/; 5. /ˈswɒləʊ/, /lɑːfs/, /lɑːfs/, /sez/

**Carelessness**
*Lines:* 1. /ˈhɒlɪdeɪ/, /ˈɔːtəm/; 2. /ˈvɪlɪdʒ/, /ˈmaʊntɪnəs/, /ˈeəriə/, /et/; 3. /ˈsɒsɪdʒɪz/, /ˈplæstɪk/, /streɪt/; 4. /kɑːnt/, /weɪst/, / /wɔːkd/; 5. /grɑːs/, /ˈkwɔːtə/, /ˈbeə/, /ˈdeɪndʒə/; 6. /ˈwɒlɪt/, /ˈpɑːspɔːt/, /ˈreɪdiəʊ/; 7. /brɑːntʃ/, /feɪld/, /ɪgˈzɔːstɪd/; 8. /tʃɑːns/, /ˈvɪlɪdʒ/; 9. /eə/ /beɪs/

135 **e**

1. ever /e/; 2. to sew /əʊ/; 3. to plead /iː/; 4. to heal /iː/; 5. jeans /iː/; 6. weight /eɪ/; 7. breakfast /e/; 8. to cheat /iː/; 9. lemon /e/; 10. leisure /e/; 11. to tear /eə/; 12. heir /eə/; 13. to search /ɜː/; 14. monkey /ɪ/

**Situational Practice**
1. /ˈiːvnɪŋ/, /kjuːɪŋ/; 2. /ˈsevrəl/, /ˈzɪərəʊ/, /hɒrɪd/, /tʃɪmni/; 3. /ˈɪntrəst/, /steɪkz/, /ˈbrekfəst/, /weɪz/, /hɑːt/, /weɪt/; 4. /səʊ/, /səkˈsiːdɪd/, /θred/; 5. /ˈiːkwəl/, /haɪt/, /ˈnaɪðə/

**My nephews**
*Lines:* 1. /ˈnefjuːz/, /ˌendʒɪˈnɪə/; 2. /kəmˈpiːt/, /kiː/, /ˈleʒə/; 3. /kəˈrɪə/, /klɑːk/, /aɪˈdɪə/; 4. /def/, /ˈrɪəli/; 5. /ˈdʒeləs/, /kəˈrɪə/; 6. /ˌlemənz/; 7. /tʃiːtɪd/, /pliːdɪd/; 8. /ˈfɒrɪn/, /ˈsɑːdʒnt/, /ˈfiːvə/, /helθ/; 9. /ˈiːvn/; 10. /ˈdʒuːəlz/, /ˈprɪti/; 11. /ˈpriːviəs/; 12. /eə/

137 **i**

1. to determine /ɪ/; 2. to live /ɪ/; 3. Christ /aɪ/; 4. idiot /ɪ/; 5. niece /iː/; 6. privilege /ɪ/

**Situational Practice**
1. /ˈkrɪstʃənz/, /kraɪst/, /ˌkrɪstiˈænəti/, /ˈkrɪsməs/
2. /paɪnts/, /ˈæpətaɪt/, /ˈmedsn/, /ɪˈmædʒɪn/, /θɜːsti/
3. /ˈbɪznəsmənz/, /ˈpraɪvət/, /pəˈliːsmən/, /ˈhæŋkəˌtʃɪf/, /ˈpaɪlət/, /ˈlaɪsns/, /ˈælɪbaɪ/, /ˈbɪznəsmənz/, /niːs/
4. /aɪˈdɪə/, /ˈeɪnʃnt/, /ˌmægəˈziːnz/, /ˈsaɪəns/, /məˈʃiːnz/, /ˈpɑːləmənt/, /ˈfaɪnlz/, /ˈaɪtəmz/

139

### o

1. toe /əʊ/; 2. improve /uː/; 3. gone /ɒ/; 4. blood /ʌ/; 5. to worry /ʌ/; 6. county /aʊ/; 7. to show /əʊ/; 8. abroad /ɔː/; 9. coach /əʊ/; 10. cough /ɒ/; 11. company /ʌ/; 12. host /əʊ/; 13. progress /əʊ/; 14. comb /əʊ/; 15. southern /ʌ/; 16. knowledge /ɒ/

**Situational Practice**
1. /'mʌŋki/, /'nɒnsəns/
2. /'kʌmpəni/, /kraʊd/, /blʌd/
3. /bəʊsts/, /gəʊlkipə/, /'prəʊgres/, /'nɒlɪdʒ/
4. /ʃuːz/, /blaʊzɪz/, /'mɒdl/, /'taʊəlz/, /kəʊm/, /daʊt/, /'wʊmən/

**The First English Colony in America**
*Lines:* 1. /'kʌmpəni/, /'pɜːpəs/, /'sʌðən/; 2. /'kɒləni/, /ə'mʌŋ/; 3. /'trʌbl/, /bəʊz/; 4. /kən'dɪʃənz/, /ɪm'pruːvd/, /kə'nuː/, /'kʌləfl/, /'prɒdʌkts/; 5. /'gʌvənd/, /'kɒləni/, /'kʌpl/, /wuːndɪd/; 6. /dʌn/, /'gʊd/, /'kɒləni/

**A Trip to the Zoo**
*Lines:* 1. /'kʌntri/; 2. /zuː/, /həʊst/, /ə'kʌmpəni/; 3. /kaʊtʃ/, /'wʌndə/; 4. /'nɒnsəns/, /wʌri/; 5. /'petrəl/, /ə'prəʊtʃd/; 6. /ə'laʊd/, /'mʌni/, /kəm'pænjənz/; 7. /'ʃaʊə/; 8. /ə'mʌŋ/, /kraʊd/, /frʌnt/; 9. /rɔː/, /nʌn/, /rɔːd/, /'mʌŋkiz/, /'stʌmək/; 10. /'trʌbl/; 11. /'dʌzən/, /'mʌŋkiz/, /ə'bʌv/; 12. /blaʊz/, /flʌdz/, /'kʌrɪdʒ/, /'mʌŋki/; 13. /bə'luːn/; 14. /kɒf/, /glʌvz/

141

### u

1. dull /ʌ/; 2. butcher /ʊ/; 3. to bury /e/; 4. guilt /ɪ/; 5. to blush /ʌ/; 6. tube /juː/; 7. puzzle /ʌ/; 8. to cure /ʊə/; 9. busy /ɪ/; 10. suburb /ʌ/; 11. sugar /ʊ/; 12. sure /ʊ/

**Situational Practice**
1. /'kʊʃn/; 2. /'juːnjənz/, /sə'pɔːt/, /'mjuːtʃuəl/; 3. /'kʌbəd/, /pɜːs/, /'bʊtʃəz/, /'suːpəˌmɑːkɪt/, /'juːʒʊəli/, /'ʃʊgə/, /'pʊdɪŋ/, /dʒuːs/, /'bʌkɪt/, /blʌʃɪz/, /hʌgz/; 4. /bʊldɒg/, /bʊʃɪz/, /'bʊlɪt/, /sə'spektɪd/, /'bɜːgləri/, /'pʌzld/, /'bʌtn/, /'bʌtlə/, /'gɪlti/, /'bʌtn/, /'bʌtləz/

**London**
*Lines:* 1. /gaɪd/, /'dɪfɪklt/; 2. /'pʌblɪk/, /sə'dʒest/, /'tjuːb/; 3. /'fɪgəz/; 4. /'lɪtrətʃə/, /berid/, /gɑːdz/; 5. /'bɪziɪst/, /kɜːv/; 6. /'lʌkʃərɪ/, /klʌbz/; 7. /'ʃʊə/, /'bɪznəsmen/, /suːts/; 8. /gɪ'tɑːz/, /pʊʃɪŋ/, /fruːt/; 9. /rʌʃ/, /'sʌbɜːbz/; 10. /dʌl/, /'ʌgli/

## 2. Consonants

143

### g

1. gear /g/; 2. singer /ŋ/; 3. anger /ŋ/; 4. angel /dʒ/; 5. legal /g/; 6. daughter /–/; 7. garage /ʒ/; 8. rough /f/

**Situational Practice**
1. /streɪndʒə/, /'dʒɜːmən/, /'ɪŋglənd/, /streɪndʒə/
2. /rʌf/, /'pæsɪdʒ/, /'ɪŋglɪʃ/, /'dʒaɪənt/, /ɪg'zædʒəˌreɪtɪŋ/, /'pæsɪndʒəz/
3. /ɪ'mædʒɪn/, /mə'dʒɪʃən/, /'pɪdʒnz/, /fɪŋgəz/, /mædʒɪk/
4. /'dʒenrəl/ /ˌledʒɪ'sleɪʃn/, /'ɒrɪdʒɪn/
5. /ɪ'nʌf/, /'hæŋəz/, /sɪŋə/, /mænɪdʒə/
6. /elɪgəntli/, /'dʒenjuɪn/
7. 'lɑːfɪŋ/, /'dɔːtə/, /drɑːft/; /kɔːt/
8. /'hʌŋgə/, /θɪŋ/

145

## ch

1. arch /tʃ/; 2. scheme /k/; 3. chief /tʃ/; 4. technical /k/; 5. spinach /tʃ/

**Situational Practice**
1. /'stʌməkeɪk/, /'stʌmək/, /ti:tʃə/, /hedeɪk/
2. /mɪ'kænɪk/, /mə'ʃi:n/
3. /'kɔ:rəs/, /'ɑ:kɪtekt/, /ski:m/, /rɪtʃ/, /'ʃeʊfɜ:/
4. /mɑ:tʃ/, /ɪntʃɪz/

147

## s, x

1. please /z/; 2. jealousy /s/; 3. treasure /ʒ/; 4. result /z/; 5. issue /ʃ/; 6. husband /z/; 7. please /z/; 8. disease /z/; 9. excuse /ks/; 10. suit /s/

**Situational Practice**
1. /'tenʃn/, /'ʃʊgə/, /'beɪsn/
2. /si:st/, /ɪg'zɪst/, /pə'zeʃn/, /dɪ'zɒlvd/, /fɔ:ls/
3. /'hʌzbəndz/, /dɪ'zɑ:stə/, /'meʒəz/, /dɪ'zɒlv/, /rɪ'zʌlt/, /dɪ'zi:z/, /si:st/, /'penʃn/, /'ɪŋkri:s/, /'tju:zdeɪz/, /'wenzdeɪz/, /'θɜ:zdeɪz/, /ʃɔ:/, /'sɒsɪdʒɪz/, /'pleʒə/, /tʃeɪsɪŋ/, /'treʒə/, /'epɪsəʊdz/, /ˌkjʊəri'ɒsəti/, /kəm'pærɪsn/, /ɪg'zædʒəreɪtɪd/, /'dʒeləsi/, /'sɪzəz/
4. /ju:st/, /ɪk'skju:sɪz/, /ju:zd/, /ju:st/

147

## th

**Situational Practice**
1. /bɑ:θ/, /beɪð/, /smu:ð/
2. /bri:ðɪŋ/, /breθ/, /wɜ:ði/
3. /'nɔ:ðnə/, /'sʌðən/, /nɔ:θ/, /saʊθ/

149

## Silent Consonants

1. /'wenzdeɪ/, /bɒm/, /'sentə/, /'θɪətə/, /'vi:ɪkl/, /'krɪsməs/
2. /'aɪlənd/, /kɑ:m/, /nɒt/, /fɑ:sən/, /'hænsm/, /lɪmz/, /'mʌslz/, /ɪg'zɔ:stɪd/
3. /'lɪsn/, /ʃʊdnt/, /'wɪsl/, /mʌsnt/, /'sændwɪdʒɪz/, /dʌm/
4. /dets/, /daʊt/, /klaɪm/, /det/

## 3. Different Pronunciation of Words of Similar Spelling

149

1. /beə/, /bɪəd/, /bɪə/, /'bʊtʃə/; 2. /'bʌtləz/; 3. /kɔ:z/, /kɔ:s/; 4. /'kʌstəm/, /'kɒstju:mz/; 5. /'mʌŋki/, /'dɒŋki/; 6. /dʒeɪl/, /gəʊlz/; 7. /lu:s/, /lu:z/; 8. /meə/, /'meɪdʒə/; 9. /pɔ:/, /pjʊə/, /pɔ:/; 10. /pə'teɪtəʊz/, /tə'mɑ:təʊz/; 11. /səʊp/, /su:p/; 12. /swi:t/, /swet/; 13. /tju:nz/, /təʊn/; 14. /tʌŋ/; 15. /'wʌndə/, /'wɒndəd/

# WORTREGISTER

Die Ziffern geben die Seiten an.
Zusammenziehungen, Abkürzungen und Wörter, die nur als Beispiele zur Erläuterung einer Regel dienen, sind im Allgemeinen nicht in das Wortregister aufgenommen.
Verbformen erscheinen unter dem Infinitiv.

# SACHREGISTER

Die Ziffern geben die Seiten an.